K. L. Alston

"CHANGE, IT'S SIMPLER THAN YOU THINK!"

Published by K. L. Alston Enterprises

No part of this publication may be reproduced, stored in a retrieval system or transmitted in any form or by any means, electronic, mechanical, photocopying, recording, scanning or otherwise, except under the terms of the Copyright, Designs and Patent Act without prior written approval by the author. Requests to the author for permission should be addressed to K. L. Alston Enterprises by visiting www.klalston.com via E-mail at klalston@klalston.com

Copyright © 2011 United States Copyright Office
ALL RIGHTS RESERVED

Published May 2011
K.L. Alston Enterprises

ISBN-10 0-9796482-3-8
ISBN-13 978-0-9796482-3-6

For information about K. L. Alston Enterprises or to order more copies of this book, please visit
www.klalston.com

"Your beliefs come with the power of life or death. Your beliefs can empower and propel you to excellent health, wealth and true happiness. Or, your beliefs can keep you unhealthy, poor and miserable. You choose." K. L. Alston

Dedicated to

My Family and Friends!

Table of Contents

Acknowledgement .... Page 4
Introduction .... Page 6
Chapter 1: *Do You Truly Desire a Better Quality of Life?* .... Page 9
Chapter 2: *The "WHY" and "HOW" of Behaviors* .... Page 14
Chapter 3: *Forming and Breaking Habits (Behaviors)* .... Page 20
Chapter 4: *Delayed Gratification (The Stanford Marshmallow Experiment)* .... Page 64
Chapter 5: *7 Natural Laws* .... Page 73
Chapter 6: *Life Is Dynamic; Not Static* .... Page 85
Chapter 7: Conclusion .... Page 98
About Our Logo .... Page 101

Exercise 1: .... Page 26
Exercise 2: .... Page 28
Exercise 3: .... Page 43
Exercise 4: .... Page 44
Exercise 5: .... Page 48
Exercise 6: .... Page 49
Exercise 7: .... Page 62
Exercise 8: .... Page 69
Exercise 9: .... Page 70
Exercise 10: .... Page 71
Exercise 11: .... Page 72
Exercise 12: .... Page 83
Exercise 13: .... Page 83
Exercise 14: .... Page 94
Exercise 15: .... Page 95
Exercise 16: .... Page 96
Exercise 17: .... Page 97

Introduction

If any image truly represents the perfect analogy when it comes to what is occurring with us internally (Subconsciously) and externally (Consciously), it's an iceberg. On the surface everything may appear peaceful and serene; however, this is only 10% of the picture. The remaining 90% is beneath the surface and this is where the majority of the activity occurs.

In this book, we will explore the concepts of behavior and change from the inside (Subconscious) out (Conscious) and you will learn the strategies required to immediately change or get rid of behaviors that are self-defeating and disempowering. By truly understanding what is occurring subconsciously and consciously, you will become fully capable of smoothly transitioning from a position of feeling helpless and controlled to a position of being empowered and in control.

"CHANGE,
IT'S SIMPLER THAN YOU THINK!"

Chapter 1

Do You Truly Desire a Better Quality of Life?

Do you truly desire a better quality of life? Are you finally tired of being tired? Since you are reading this book, I'm willing to bet you do and you are. You're searching for answers and you are at the right place at the right time with the right tool (this book) in your hand(s). To get you started, here's the best place to start ... let's start working on you. Too much time and energy is wasted attempting to change something that is extremely difficult to change ... someone else. A lot less time and energy is wasted when you place your focus on changing yourself than when you focus your time and energy on attempting to change someone else. Plus, it's amazing how your entire outlook changes when you have made the necessary adjustments in your own behavior.

I remember during a management class I was taking to complete my Masters degree, the professor was teaching from a PowerPoint® presentation. He displayed a slide that stated people, in general, would rather stay in an environment that is overwhelmingly negative than to change their current environment or even attempt to change their current environment. I processed that one slide for quite awhile thinking about what it had stated. It then dawned on me why that statement held so much truth … CHANGE. Most people are afraid of change; therefore, they would rather stay in an environment that is overwhelmingly negative because although this may be the case, they are familiar with it and they know what to expect from it. Implementing change would present a variable called 'the unknown' which, in most individuals, brings on a feeling of fear.

Well, change will always be a factor and choosing to be miserable and unhappy for the sake of attempting to avoid change is not the answer. This book provides you with strategies and exercises that will impact the manner in which you think, react, respond and derive at decisions from an internal perspective generating successful change that is driven from the inside out and eliminating that fear of 'the unknown' because you will be in total control of the change that is taking place.

Beginning in this first chapter you will realize this book is not about life as usual, it's about changing lives. During the writing of this book, a moment of reflection caused me to realize that my life consisted of quite a few decisions and behaviors that were made and exhibited without fully analyzing the situation and becoming more familiar with the variables that were involved; that led to sometimes, more times than not, making decisions or exhibiting behaviors that were not always best suited for the situation. But why did I make the decisions I made or exhibited the behavior I did in the first place and what were the driving forces behind those actions?

Over the years, I've had the opportunity and privilege of working along side and sharing thoughts, methodologies and strategies with some of the most brilliant and successful people in the realms of personal self-development and self-mastery. In the pages of this book, I share with you information, strategies and exercises that have completely transformed my life as well as the lives of countless others. The exercises are by far the most important part of this book. Reason being, "What you **Hear**, you forget. What you **See**, you remember. What you **Do**, you understand!" All too often, books are read and no change takes place. In most cases, this is not due to a poorly written book. It's a result of the reader not applying what was presented in the book. Do not just read this book without completing the exercises. Each exercise is specifically designed to help you tap into your reservoir of infinite untapped potential; therefore, I recommend completing each exercise before continuing to the next section. The impact on you and your life will be exponentially increased if you abide by this simple request.

If you truly apply the lessons and strategies expressed in this book and with a sense of commitment complete the exercises, your life will take on an entirely new and totally different level of meaning. Every successful person I have had the opportunity to be around, learn from, interact and work with possesses an in-depth understanding of what has been laid out in this book; and they apply the strategies contained in this book consistently and this is why they live the lifestyles that they do.

Chapter 2
The "WHY" and "HOW" of Behaviors

I am intrigued with the 'why' and 'how' of behaviors. Why are the behaviors being exhibited and how can the behaviors be modified or gotten rid of if there is a desire to do so? On this journey, I have been led to the distinct understanding and appreciation that if you truly want to successfully modify or get rid of unwanted behaviors; you must first have, at a minimum, a basic understanding of why the behaviors exist and what triggers them in the first place. How can you modify or change something you have no understanding of?

I appreciate and enjoy the art and science of technology to the point where I hold an advance degree in the area. However, my appreciation and enjoyment of this discipline does not lie within the discipline itself. My appreciation lies more within the fact that information systems and technology are the closest academic disciplines I could have studied that truly emulate the functioning of the human brain and neurological system than actually studying Biology or Neurology.

We experience the world through our senses; sight, sound, touch, taste and smell. Everything we've ever learned and ever will learn is learned via our senses and although this is a basic understanding, when I began to study the neurology and psychology of learning and behavior, this basic concept and understanding took on a totally new meaning and understanding for me. We exhibit behaviors for specific reasons and those reasons are to either receive some type of pleasure from them or to relieve ourselves from some type of pain. Let's consider the behavior of an infant. When an infant is hungry, what does an infant do? The infant cries. At that point, the infant is fed. When an infant is wet, what does an infant do? The infant cries. At that point, the infant is changed. When an infant is not comfortable, what does an infant do? Yes, you guessed it. The infant cries. At that point, the infant is made to feel comforted. Although that infant is not fully consciously aware of what is going on, subconsciously that infant has learned a very simple and profound lesson; when I want what I want all I need to do is cry. Although the analogy I provided pertains to an infant, the fact of the matter is, we in general exhibit the behavior we do for the exact same reason as the infant did in the example; we want something and we want it when we want it.

The infant example is an extremely important one for you to deeply understand. Its importance lies in the fact that you must intimately beware of the fact that you began learning your behaviors from the time you were an infant (Of course science and research show that learning also takes place while in the womb before birth). So, if you have been learning your behaviors from the time you were an infant, what behaviors have you learned? There are three stages of development that science attributes to the learning of values which directly impact behavior and these periods are:

The Imprint Period which is from birth to approximately 7 years old. During this period, learning is largely subconscious and from our parents.

The Modelling Period which is from 8 years old to approximately 13 years old. During this phase, learning is largely conscious and subconscious and from copying friends.

The Socialization Period which is from 14 years old to approximately 21 years old. During this phase, the values that are learned have a great impact on the relationships that are formed afterwards.

These 3 stages of development set the stage for the rest of your live. They are that important because it is during these 3 stages that the foundation of your behavior as well as your beliefs and values and your identity are solidified.

Information Overload

Every second of the day, your senses are bombarded with over 2 million bits of information. How does your brain handle it? Interestingly enough, research shows that out of the over 2 million bits of information the senses detect every second, the brain can only process roughly 126 bits of it. That's quite a bit of information that gets lost in the translation. So, how does the brain determine what's important and what isn't? The answer to this question incorporates the 3 stages of development. The things you have been exposed to and the manner in which you have been exposed to them are very important. Your environment as well as the people, places and things that influences you all play a critical role in the information your brain detects and processes as being important and worth processing.

This book will help you to gain a solid understanding of what is occurring on the inside and what you can do to make the necessary adjustments you need to make to positively change the quality of your life by modifying or completely ridding yourself of unwanted behaviors and habits.

Chapter 3

Forming and Breaking Habits (Behaviors)

What is a habit? According to Merriam-Webster.com, a habit is defined as:

"An acquired mode of behavior that has become nearly or completely involuntary."

That definition pretty much 'hits the nail on the head', but what is really going on? Let's look beneath the surface to truly explore what is occurring. What has created it and what triggers the behavior? Let's tackle the 'what has created it' first. Habits are behaviors that have become a part of the subconscious processes. These behaviors, from a neurological perspective, have become a part of the mind and body's internal program. They are things that we have been doing for so long and we perform them so well, we no longer have to consciously think about them.

Now, these behaviors can be empowering and liberating or they can be disempowering and limiting. The fact still remains we perform them well without having to consciously think about them. This is why breaking a habit takes a conscious effort. Whenever an event or situation occurs that triggers the behavior, the reaction is involuntary because it involves chemical reactions within the brain and neurological associations that have been formed and substantiated over time. None-the-less, it's very important to understand that anything you have learned, you can unlearn.

The longer we have been exhibiting the behavior, the longer it may take to modify or completely rid ourselves of it. This is not so because the habit itself takes long, there are exercises you can do that will modify or get rid of the habit almost immediately. This is more so because of the time it takes for an individual to truly decide and commit to doing what it takes to make the transition. Making the actual decision takes less than a second, what takes time is getting to the point where you actually commit and make the decision.

Although the processing of a habit occurs subconsciously, the conscious mind can play a significant role in reference to consciously recognizing what is occurring and serving as a guide to assist the subconscious mind in the transition. Remember, it will take a conscious effort to modify or rid yourself of a behavior. Because of the subconscious nature of the behavior, when there is a reaction; that reaction may occur without you consciously realizing that you have reacted. This happens because the reaction has occurred subconsciously and so quickly, the conscious mind reacts after the behavior has been exhibited or in some cases, not at all. Have you ever did something or responded in a manner that you didn't intend to? What did you ask yourself? Maybe something like, "Why in the world did I just do that?" or "Why did I just say that?" You 'did it' or 'said it' because the event that triggered that particular behavior fired off a subconscious chain-of-events that occurred before you had the opportunity to consciously process the situation. This book will assist you with truly understanding what is occurring beneath the surface and breaking the chain-of-events to create quick and permanent change. The exercises in this book will help you make the necessary adjustments and changes so you can begin to experience the quality of life you desire.

Our Decisions Are Based Upon ...

It is important to understand that you respond to any given situation according to your internal blueprint of the world. And, there are very specific variables that contribute to that blueprint. Variables such as your identify which defines who you believe you are, your value and belief systems, your attitude, things you have experienced and your cultural beliefs. All of these variables play a huge part in shaping who you are and how you interpret the world around you.

You have become subconsciously competent regarding how you respond when these variables are in play because of the neurological associations that have been created in your brain; therefore, based upon the event, acting and reacting is not something that will necessarily involve your conscious mind. So, when a decision has to made, unless you are consciously aware and in-tune with what you are doing and what needs to be done, you will continue to make the same decision as you did in the past when dealing with that particular event.

In order to modify a habitual behavior, you have to become consciously aware of it either while it's occurring or before it occurs. How do you accomplish this? One way is by fully understanding the "red flags" or "triggers" that initiate or precede the behavior. You can then begin to consciously modify the behavior by making adjustments to the events that lead up to it and then by making different decisions than before.

This is very important so reread this section if you have to. It is critically important that you fully understand this to be able to successfully implement change in any given situation. Truly understanding why you exhibit any form of behavior from a neurological and psychological perspective empowers you with the knowledge and understanding you need to develop a plan for successful change. If necessary, again please reread this section because this chapter sets the stage for the remaining chapters. Fully understanding this chapter and then applying the strategies and techniques provided in this book will create the change you desire.

Exercise 1: Determining the Trigger

In the space provided below, write down a situation when you reacted or responded in a manner you didn't intent to.

_____

_____

_____

_____

_____

_____

_____

_____

_____

_____

_____

_____

_____

Now, write down what actually triggered your reaction or response. What was going on right before the reaction or response?

Exercise 2: Modifying or Getting Rid of Unwanted Behaviors (Note: *This strategy is based on Anthony Robbins' Neuro-Associative Conditioning (NAC) strategy which was developed by Anthony Robbins)*

In the space provided below, write down 3 behaviors you desire to rid yourself of.

_____
_____
_____
_____
_____
_____
_____
_____
_____
_____
_____
_____

Now, from the 3, choose and write down the behavior you desire to rid yourself of the most.

_____

_____

_____

Follow the 6 steps outlined below with the behavior you have chosen.

Step 1

Decide you truly desire to rid yourself of this behavior and determine what is currently preventing you from doing it.

Step 2

Provide leverage for yourself by associating and disassociating yourself with the behavior. Visualize yourself (associating) exhibiting the behavior. Also, visualize someone else (dissociating) exhibiting the behavior as you're standing there watching how unproductive the behavior actually is.

You have to create a sense of urgency in reference to ridding yourself of the behavior. Visualize all the ways in which this behavior is costing you something that you truly desire to have. Visualize the pain and discomfort that can come from this behavior and how it is limiting you in reference to accomplishing something critically important to you.

Step 3

As you are visualizing the behavior, interrupt the pattern of the behavior by doing something unexpected. (*For example, if you normally get angry if someone cuts you off in traffic, instead of getting angry, burst out laughing.*) Replay the behavior in reverse really fast. Change the picture of the visualization to something that is more pleasant to you. Perform these routines a dozen or more times to break the existing behavioral pattern.

Step 4

Create a new and empowering alternative behavior to replace the limiting behavior you just ridded yourself of.

Step 5

Condition the new and empowering behavior until is becomes consistent. Continue to repeat the behavior utilizing all of your senses (Sight, Sound, Touch, Taste and Smell) to experience the new and empowering behavior.

Setup a schedule to reinforce the new and empowering behavior. Think of all the ways this new behavior will help you get what you want. Think of all the great rewards that will come from you exhibiting the new and empowering behavior and reward yourself for it.

Step 6

Test the new behavior for effectiveness and ecology. You have to make sure that the change in behavior is going to impact your life in a positive way and that it is in alignment with your beliefs, values and rules.

In order to modify or get rid of a behavior, it is very important to know what triggers the behavior and Exercise 1 will help you figure that out. You can then utilize Exercise 2 to rid yourself of any limiting or disempowering behavior. You can use these exercises for any behavior you desire to modify or get rid of.

Let's continue your journey of transformation. The next stop in your journey is gaining an understanding of your conscious and subconscious minds.

The Conscious and Subconscious Minds

Your conscious mind is your short-term memory. It is the part of your brain that is aware of things that are currently occurring or have occurred within a reasonable span of time. It is efficient and effective at storing thoughts or processes from minutes to hours. This is the part of your brain you are utilizing when you make a mental list of things you need to pickup from the super-market. You store these items in memory long enough for you to go to the super-market and purchase the items. At that point, the memory of the items is no longer necessary, therefore it is purged. Other examples are getting a phone number from someone and storing it in memory just long enough for you to find something to write it down on, or studying at the last minute and 'cramming' for an examination.

Another great comparison of how your conscious mind works in reference to storing and processing information is that of how the memory of a computer works. The term RAM (Random Access Memory) is the term that describes the short-term memory of a computer. RAM is everything you see on the computing screen as well as functions that are running in the background like the operating system when the computer is on and in use. It is called RAM because when the computer is powered off, these processes stop functioning and everything on the computer's screen goes away. If there were documents you were working on and they were not saved, they would be gone and you would have to retype them. This occurs because RAM is only short-term memory and information is not stored there for an extended period of time.

Things your conscious mind is extremely proficient at:

- Working Linearly
- Processing Sequentially
- Logic
- Verbal Language
- Mathematics
- Analysis

Your subconscious mind is your long-term memory. This is where your memories reside and these memories can be your best friend or your worst enemy. In order to gain control of you life, you have to gain control of your thinking. In order to gain control of your thinking, you have to gain control of your memories. By understanding how your subconscious mind functions, you can begin to make the necessary adjustments and changes that will align you with living a life where your past need not dictate your present nor create your future.

A great comparison of how your subconscious mind works in reference to storing and processing information would be how the long term memory of a computer works. The term ROM (Read-Only Memory) is the term that describes the long-term memory of the computer. Unlike RAM, ROM retains its content even after the computer has been powered off. So the content in ROM can be accessed again and again until it is deleted or purged. Your subconscious mind has access to all your memories and utilizes this data to make decisions involving current events.

Things your subconscious mind is extremely proficient at:

- Working Holistically
- Intuition
- Creativity

- Running Your Body
- Taking Care of Your Emotions
- Storing Memories

Processing and understanding the relationship between your memories (Subconscious) and your behavior is a very important step in gaining control of your life. In order to successfully navigate this process, here are 5 areas you must understand about your subconscious mind and how it operates:

I. Your subconscious mind does not process negatives.
II. Your subconscious mind requires direction.
III. Your subconscious mind preserves memories.
IV. Your subconscious mind is always thriving to learn.
V. Your subconscious mind behaves based upon what it has learned.

Let's explore these 5 areas in more detail.

Your Subconscious Mind Does Not Process Negatives

Your subconscious mind processes everything you think as a positive suggestion. This is an important point because so many people think that focusing on what they don't want to happen is thinking positively. Thinking, "I don't want to be poor" is not the same as thinking, "I will be wealthy". For example, if I say "Don't think about a pink elephant, what do you think about? Since the subconscious mind does not process negatives, if you are thinking, "I don't want to be poor", the subconscious mind processes it as if you're suggesting "I want to be poor". This is the reason why it is vitally important for you to always state your goals in the affirmative.

Your Subconscious Mind Needs Direction

It can be extremely dangerous to allow your subconscious mind to just roam freely. It needs to be guided. This is the purpose of your conscious mind; providing guidance for the subconscious mind. And, if this guidance does not occur, the subconscious mind will find it wherever it can. I can remember my grandmother always saying, "An idle mind is the devil's workshop." Your subconscious mind is like a tape recorder that plays back the events (memories) that are stored in it; therefore, there has to be an open line of communication between the subconscious mind and the conscious mind. This open line of communication can be established via meditation and during times of deep relaxation.

Your Subconscious Mind Preserves Memories

One of the functions of the subconscious mind is to suppress memories with unresolved negative emotions. The subconscious mind then has the function of presenting these suppressed memories for examination so that any trapped emotions can be released. This is one reason why it is important that you are consciously aware of what is happening on the inside because suppressed memories can manifest themselves at the blink of an eye in the form of a behavior or a reaction and if not checked by the conscious mind, this manifesting can occur at the most inopportune time.

Your Subconscious Mind Is Always Thriving To Learn

Your subconscious mind is always looking to learn new things. It's important that you are consistently exposing yourself to new things that are producing positive results. This statement will make more sense after you read the next point below. It's up to you to consciously find constructive things to do to keep your subconscious mind occupied. Because if not, it will find things to get into and these things may not be in your best interest. Activities such as reading, exercising and meditation are great because not only do they put you in a better state of mind, they also keep you mentally fit by producing growth in the brain cells and dendrites (branches of a brain cell).

Your Subconscious Mind Behaves Based Upon What It Has Learned

This is one of the most important things you must understand about your subconscious mind, it will keep you on the path of whatever it has been programmed to do. What ever you have permitted your subconscious mind to inherit; it will force it back upon you. This is one of the reasons why a terrorist can kill and destroy without guilt. This individual truly believes he is being a moral person and fighting for something worth dying for. On the other hand, if an individual does something that is not 'in the norm' of what his/her subconscious mind renders appropriate; this individual may experience extreme guilt or even pain. The guilt or pain is a result of the individual's subconscious mind punishing them for a behavior that is not a part of their normal character. This is why beliefs, values, one's identity and their environment play a major role in their development on a subconscious level.

The thing I want you to fully understand is any behavior that has been learned can be unlearned. It is called change. Your thoughts and your feelings create your life. Whatever you are thinking and feeling at any given moment is dictating your present and creating your future. The only meaning of anything is the meaning you assign to it.

Exercise 3: For 5 minutes, make a list of the beliefs you have that empower you.

Exercise 4: From your list above (Exercise 3), highlight the top 3 beliefs that empower you and answer the following questions:

How do these beliefs empower me?

_____

_____

_____

_____

_____

_____

_____

_____

_____

_____

_____

_____

_____

How do these beliefs strengthen me?

How do these beliefs motivate me?

Exercise 5: For 5 minutes, make a list of the beliefs you have that are disempowering to you.

Exercise 6: From your list above (Exercise 5), highlight the top 2 beliefs that are disempowering to you and answer the following questions:

What are these beliefs costing me?

_____

_____

_____

_____

_____

_____

_____

_____

_____

_____

_____

_____

How are these beliefs preventing me from accomplishing my desired goals?

How are these beliefs ridiculous?

_____

_____

_____

Exercises 3, 4, 5 and 6 will help you to identity beliefs you have that are beneficial to you and beliefs you have that are not beneficial to you. Once you have identified which beliefs are which, you are now in a better position to rid yourself of disempowering and self-sabotaging beliefs by recognizing what is triggering them and how you can modify or get rid of them (Strategies Learned in Exercises 1 and 2).

Let's look at the stages of how a behavior becomes a habit. There are so many different theories that scientists and researchers as well as scholars have come up with that describe life and how we react to it. The Four Stages of Learning lays it out quite simply and is a simple concept that will lead to a deeper understanding of how the subconscious mind receives it programs and how you can begin to create change.

The Four Stages of Learning are:

1. Subconsciously Incompetence
2. Conscious Incompetence
3. Conscious Competence
4. Subconscious Competence

To explain these Four Stages, I will utilize the analogy of learning how to drive an automobile. This is something that most can relate to. When a person initially begins to learn how to drive, he/she is ***Subconsciously Incompetent***, meaning they have no idea what they are doing. They don't know the gas pedal from the brake pedal; where to place their hands on the steering wheel; or how to keep the car going straight. There is definitely a lack of understanding in reference to how much pressure to apply to the gas pedal and how to find the brake pedal quickly and smoothly.

As the person gets more and more lessons under his/her belt, there is a greater level of comfort. This person has become ***Consciously Incompetent***, meaning they have become consciously aware of what to do; however, there is still quite a bit of learning going on in reference to doing it with confidence and finesse. Although the gas and brake pedals are no longer strangers, the person is still learning how to apply the appropriate amount of pressure to each to get the desired results ... smooth starting and stopping.

It's now several months later and the person is driving much better now. He/she understands the laws of the road and has become quite adept at applying pressure to the gas pedal and to the break pedal. The person is now able to steer the automobile exceptionally well and has now even received his/her state driver's license. This person has now become ***Consciously Competent***, meaning they are now able to perform all the necessary functions to operate a vehicle safely and responsibly. However, there is still some mental processing going on when operating the automobile.

Finally, this person has been driving for years. He/she is now operating a vehicle without having to think much about it. As a matter of fact, he/she can, while driving, be on the cell phone via a blue tooth having a conversation with a friend. At the same time, he/she can make the necessary adjustments to the volume of the radio while simultaneously deciding if the best turn is the right turn coming up or the left turn at the next block. This person has become ***Subconsciously Competent***, meaning driving for him/her has become second nature.

Although I utilized learning how to drive to illustrate the Four Stages of Learning, these stages apply to anything you have learned to do well over time. This includes things that are not necessarily in your best interest. When it comes to things you have been doing for quite sometime, you are *subconsciously competent*. In other words, these things have become habitual to you. The question is, "Are those things good habits are not so good habits?"

So how do you unlearn the behaviors (habits) you need to modify or rid yourself of? The answer is quite simple, but the process takes effort and a willingness to do something different. Just as it took time for the behavior to become a habit, it is going to take some time for you to unlearn that behavior. The great news is; you can unlearn them in much less time by simply applying the strategies in this book alone.

How do you do it? You have to reverse the process and go from being *Subconsciously Competent* back to being *Consciously Competent*. Any behavior you exhibit that you are *Subconsciously Competent* with pretty much occurs on autopilot. You naturally don't have to think about it to perform it. In order to go from being *Subconsciously Competent* back to being *Consciously Competent,* you have to start consciously thinking about how that behavior manifests itself. You have to physically process and physically write down the set of events that occur prior to the behavior manifesting itself *(See Exercise 1).*

This is very important because it is much easier to unlearn a behavior when you consciously understand why the behavior is occurring in the first place. Once you begin to make yourself aware of the behavior prior to and while it is occurring, you can begin to replace that behavior with a more favorable behavior or rid yourself of it completely.

Here is the science and the art of the entire process. From a neurological perspective, when you begin to consciously modify a behavior, the neuro-associations that have formed begin to weaken. The more you don't exhibit the behavior or reinforce the associations, the weaker the neuro-associations become until the associations are completely gone. The severing of the neuro-associations is what actually modifies the behavior or completely gets rid of it depending upon what your desired outcome is.

You can now create a new behavior by creating a new set of neuro-associations that reinforce the new behavior with references that positively substantiate the new behavior. The once *Subconsciously Competent* "not so good" behavior you were exhibiting has now been replaced with a new and better behavior that will become a *Subconsciously Competent* behavior. This is why it is so important to be mindful of your environment and whom you allow to influence you. All beliefs which directly impact behavior are a result of neuro-associations that have been formed over time and have been substantiated and reinforced by references that validate that belief as being important and true to you.

It is very important to mention here that although the old habit has been modified or gotten rid of, if one is not careful, he/she can find themselves back in that old habit exhibiting that same old behavior. This is why you have to test the new behavior and check it against your overall beliefs, values and rules. The new behavior has to fit your ecology and has to be something that is effective for you. *(See Exercise 2)*

Habits and behaviors are all about the neuro-associations that are taking place within the brain. If you will practice and apply the strategies outlined in this book along with demonstrating the discipline and focus it will take, change will occur and it will occur quickly. The question is; who wants to invest that kind of time and energy to make such positive changes? Things in society are moving extremely fast today and people want what they want when they want it. And, they want it as quickly as possible with the least amount of effort on their part. That being stated, I can tell you who wants to invest that kind of time and energy; the person who truly desires success in every arena of his/her life; the person who intimately understands and is willing to delay gratification and to do what others will not do today so that he/she will live the lifestyle that most will never live tomorrow. This is who is willing to invest the time and the energy to make the necessary modifications to their behavior.

Exercise 7: Think of a behavior you exhibit automatically that you desire to modify. Consciously think about it and in the space provided below, write down each step you perform leading up to exhibiting that particular behavior.

_____
_____
_____
_____
_____
_____
_____
_____
_____
_____
_____
_____
_____

_____

_____

_____

_____

_____

_____

_____

This exercise helps you to consciously process what you are doing prior to a habitual behavior occurring. Once you have put the process in writing, you will now be able to go back to the consciously competent phase of that behavior and make the necessary modifications by applying the strategies you have already learned in this book.

Chapter 4

Delayed Gratification (The Stanford Marshmallow Experiment)

In the previous section, I mentioned delaying gratification. This is an important concept in reference to accomplishing dreams and goals. Delayed gratification is not just haphazardly denying yourself the things you want. It is a systematic process that involves making strategic decisions in reference to the opportunity costs of a given decision. An opportunity cost is anything that is given up in order to achieve something else. The result of your being willing to give something up should be the positioning of yourself to receive something better. The experiment below performed by Walter Mischel during the 1960s captures the importance of delayed gratification.

During the 1960s, a psychologist by the name of Walter Mischel conducted an experiment utilizing a group of 4 year olds. He gave each child a marshmallow and instructed them if they don't eat the marshmallow and wait for him to return to the room in 20 minutes, he would reward them with another marshmallow for being patient. Some of the children immediately ate their marshmallow while a number of the children were able to delay the gratification by resisting temptation as they waited.

Fourteen years later, Walter Mischel followed up on the children from the experiment and what he found out was truly fascinating. The children who could not wait and ate their marshmallow immediately:

I. *Suffered from Low Self Esteem.*
II. *Were regarded by their teachers and parents as being stubborn.*

> III. *Were susceptible to envy and easily frustrated.*

While the children who were able to restrain themselves were:

> I. *Self-Motivated*
> II. *Successful in the Classroom.*
> III. *Possessed Higher Emotional Intelligence.*

The experiment showed that individuals who are able to delay gratification for better returns stand a better chance of living a more positive life. So in essence, "patience is a virtue", but how do we incorporate it into our lives on a daily basis when we are bombarded with so many different things?

During the experiment, some children were reported as covering their eyes so that they could not see the marshmallow in front of them. That was a very good strategy because if they could not see the marshmallow, the temptation of wanting to eat it would not be there. That's one thing we could do to avoid the temptation of something; remove it from our presence. It has been scientifically proven that one of the worse times to go shopping is when you are hungry. When you do this, there is a tendency to spend more.

Another child reportedly licked the table around the marshmallow in the attempt to wait until the time has passed. This is also another good strategy; finding an alternative that is just as satisfying. I can imagine the 4 year old licking the desk around the marshmallow. I still smile when I think about that, but it worked. The child was able to delay the gratification until the time had expired.

And finally, focus on the reward. Definitely having two marshmallows is better than having only one. Some of the children were able to hold out based on the fact that they would rather have two than one. You want to purchase a new home, but don't quite have all the money you need just yet. You see this nice new car you want and you do have the money for it; however, this money is the money you have to go towards your new home. Which one is more important? Do you delay the gratification of purchasing the new car in order to be able to purchase the new home you have always wanted or do you get the car?

Exercise 8: In the space provided, write the top 5 decisions you are currently faced with making.

_____

_____

_____

_____

_____

_____

_____

_____

_____

_____

_____

_____

_____

_____

_____

Exercise 9: Out of the top 5 decisions you wrote down, in the space provided below, pick the top 3 decisions and write them down.

_____

_____

_____

_____

_____

_____

_____

_____

_____

_____

_____

_____

Exercise 10: For the top 3 decisions you wrote down, in the space provided below, write down **all** the options you believe are available to you in regards to these top 3 decisions and write them down.

_____

_____

_____

_____

_____

_____

_____

_____

_____

_____

_____

_____

_____

_____

_____

_____

_____

_____

_____

Exercise 11: Study all the options you have written down and then determine the pros and cons of each option. Decide which options will make the most sense by determining which ones present the best rewards for each decision.

These exercises (Exercises 8, 9, 10 and 11) will help you make the transition from being a problem-thinker to being a problem-solver.

Chapter 5

7 Natural Laws

According to Merriam-Webster.com, a law is defined as:

"A rule of conduct or action prescribed or formally recognized as binding or enforced by a controlling authority."

There are 7 natural laws that if understood and applied will assist you with transforming your life into the life you desire and the life you deserve. Those 7 Natural Laws are:

1. *The Law of Perpetual Transmutation*
2. *The Law of Relativity*
3. *The Law of Vibration and Attraction*
4. *The Law of Polarity*
5. *The Law of Rhythm*
6. *The Law of Cause and Effect*

7. *The Law of Gender*

Let's examine them more closely.

The Law of Perpetual Transmutation – <u>This law expresses that energy moves into physical form.</u>

The images and perceptions you hold in your mind most often materialize as results in your life. This is the concept of you visualizing your dreams and goals and believing you will have what you desire even though physically you may not at that point. It comes down to your belief system.

What are the types of things you think about the majority of the time? Does the least little thing throws you off-track and causes you to be less positive in your thinking and outlook regarding everything else? On a daily basis, we are bombarded with all sorts of stuff, some of them good and some of them not-so-good. The great news is; we get to choose those things we want to focus on. If thinking about a not-so-good situation causes you to feel bad the majority of the time and thinking about a good situation causes you to feel good the majority of the time, then it makes more logical sense to think more about the good things. So, why is there so much focus on the not-so-good? Remember Chapter 3 suitably entitled, ***"Forming and Breaking Habits"?*** Thinking negatively is also an habitual behavior. There are people who find it much easier to find and **<u>focus on</u>** the negative aspects of a situation no matter what the situation is. And, they are comfortable with this behavior, although it's causing them discomfort. They are much more comfortable with this approach than they are with taking the necessary steps to rid themselves of that behavior. The reason for their level of comfort ... the process involves change. Most people would rather remain in a stressful environment that is causing them all sorts of stress than to implement change because, although the current environment may be stressful, they are familiar with it and know what it is. To invoke change means to take a step into the unknown. The majority of people are not willing to do that and that is why going the extra mile is so important.

There was a time when it seemed I never had enough money to go around. I ran out of money before I ran out of month. If permitted, this could be extremely frustrating especially when you're working all day and it doesn't appear you are making 'ends-meet' so to speak. The majority of the time, I was focusing on the money I did not have to go around and what I could not pay and this was creating a very stressful lifestyle for me. Then one day, I got tired of being frustrated and 'stressed-out' over money and what I thought was a lack thereof. I decided to focus on what finances I did have which made me focus more on how I was spending the finances I did have which forced me to become more financially responsible.

Let's process the chain-of-events that took place. I went from being frustrated and 'stressed-out' to being not frustrated and not 'stressed-out' because I made a positive adjustment to a single thought pertaining to only one aspect of my life. My financial situation did not change until my perception of my financial situation changed. When I focused on the finances I didn't have the majority of the time, I didn't have it the majority of the time. However, when I focused on the finances I did have the majority of the time; my perception of my financial situation changed for the better which eventually lead to more money physically coming into my life. Since I was appreciative and managed a little as though it were a lot, I was then blessed with more.

"You have the authority to choose what you will focus on and how it will impact your life!" K. L. Alston

The Law of Relativity – <u>This law expresses that nothing exists unless it can be related to something else.</u>

There is no such thing as a good day unless you can relate it to a bad day. Nothing is big unless it is related to something small. Sometimes when you are experiencing a difficult time or situation in your life, you may feel as if you are the only person in the world going through it. This is a normal tendency; however, by practicing relating your situation to a situation that is much worse than yours, this will help your situation appear to be much smaller than you initially perceived it to be.

This is an extremely important concept to grasp and begin to apply. Everything in our lives we understand and hold true *(Our Belief System)* is a result of learned behavior. When are experiencing something we have never experienced before, the first thing our brain attempts to do is to relate it to something similar we have experienced before. There are two very important concepts that are the driving forces behind your behavior at any given point and time and those two forces are your current state of mind *(Current State)* and your perception *(Blue Print)* of how you believe your live should be.

The Law of Vibration and Attraction – <u>This law expresses that things are constantly in motion.</u>

Everything has a vibration; therefore, nothing is truly at rest. When you are consciously aware of that vibration, you relate that to feeling. Your thoughts control your current state of mind and your blueprint dictates what you think your life should be at any given time. This has an impact on the vibration you emit. Sometimes when you are not feeling good, just becoming aware of what is dominating your thinking at that time will help you feel better.

The Law of Polarity – <u>This law expresses that everything has an opposite.</u>

Everything has an opposite: Up – Down … Night – Day. Always try to find the good in a bad situation. No matter how bad the situation may be, there is always some good in it. On the contrary, no matter how good a situation may be, there is always some bad in it.

The Law of Rhythm – <u>This law expresses that there is a rhythm to life.</u>

There is an order to life; day comes after night or a low tide follows a high tide. It is important to learn and understand the rhythms that occur in your life. When things are going well, make sure you make the most of those good times so that you can be prepared for not-so-good times. If times are bad, keep you head up and realize that it will not be bad forever, good times are coming.

The Law of Cause and Effect – <u>This law expresses that for every action, there is an opposite and equal reaction.</u>

Always be mindful of the thoughts that occupy your mind and be especially mindful of the words that come out of your mouth. Whatever you send out into the universe comes back. Treat others in the manner in which you desire to be treated and never overly concern yourself with what's in it for you or what you will get out of a situation. Just concentrate on what you can give and be extremely grateful and thankful for the positive you receive.

The Law of Gender – <u>This law expresses that every seed has an incubation period.</u>

Understand that every thought or idea you invest energy and belief into is a seed that will eventually come into physical fruition. This will happen when the time is right. All you have to do is know that it will. Sometimes you may tend to become frustrated because something you desire has not manifested itself yet. This only makes the process take longer. The moment you become frustrated and impatient, those negative feelings begin to negatively impact your state of mind which creates a chain-reaction throughout your entire being.

Exercise 12: For 7 days, at the end of each day, write down one thing that went well and one thing that didn't go well.

_____

_____

_____

_____

_____

_____

_____

Exercise 13: Then write down the answer to the following question for each thing you wrote down above, "How did I create each of these situations?

_____

_____

_____
_____
_____
_____
_____
_____
_____
_____
_____
_____
_____
_____
_____
_____
_____

These exercises (Exercise 12 and 13) will keep you accountable for your life and make you aware of the strategies that are working and the ones that are not working.

Chapter 6

Life Is Dynamic; Not Static

Life is constantly changing from moment to moment. Just as time doesn't stand still, nor does life. The 4 lines of the abbreviated form of *"The Prayer of Serenity"* are among some of the most powerful combination of words we have to live by today.

"The Prayer of Serenity"

"God grant the serenity

to accept the things I cannot change;

courage to change the things I can;

and the wisdom to know the difference."

The abbreviated form above is the most widely known of this prayer. I can remember my grandmother having a framed copy of it on the wall in her living room. Being transparent, I did not give it much thought early on in my life. However, as I became older and wiser, the power of this seemingly simple prayer took on an entirely different meaning to me. Let's break each line down and process the power within its words.

God grant me the Serenity to accept the things I cannot change … Grant me the tranquility, the stillness, the peacefulness to accept the things I cannot change. ***God grant me the Courage to change the things I can***… Grant me the bravery, the nerve, the guts to change the things I can. ***God grant me the Wisdom to know the difference***… Grant me the insight, the intelligence, the good judgment to know the difference.

Some people exert a tremendous amount of time and energy attempting to change things they cannot change at that time and the things they can change go unnoticed or untouched. *"The wisdom to know the difference"* is the critical component when it comes to not just existing but truly and holistically living!

Why? In life, things are constantly changing. Life is dynamic not static. There maybe things occurring right now in your life that no matter what you do, you will not be able to change them. But a minute, an hour, or a day later, those things that were once unchangeable have become things you can change at that moment. In comparison, there maybe things in your life right now that you can change, but a minute, an hour, or a day from now, those things that was once changeable have become things you can not change at that moment; the wisdom to know when each of these times exists is life changing.

In their book *"A 2nd Helping of Chicken Soup for the Soul"*, Jack Canfield and Mark Victor Hansen tell the following short story:

"One day, in the heat of June, a group of men were in the fields gathering the harvest. They had risen with the sun and laboured hard all day long. None had eaten since the previous evening and a massive hunger was upon them. As dusk was descending they began describing all the foods they would be eating and how big their feasts would be.

Among them one young man said nothing. Eventually the harvesters asked if his silence meant that he was not hungry. He smiled and nodded that he was not hungry. After several more hours of labour they all sat down to eat. The young man piled his plate higher than the others and started eating with great zeal. They all looked at him in amazement and reminded him that not so long ago he said he was not hungry. He smiled and said that it was not wise to be hungry when there was no food around."

This story perfectly illustrates the importance of knowing when you have the ability to change something from when you don't. The young man in the story perfectly understood that he could not change his situation at the time so focusing on being hungry was not beneficial. As the other men began talking about all the different foods they were going to eat, the young man focused his attention on what he could impact at that time which was the work his was performing. However, when it was time to eat, he clearly focused on eating and nothing else.

"But There's Time ..."

Out of all the things in life we can get back if we lose them, time is not one of them. Stop wasting precious time. Your life may not be easy and sometimes it may not appear to be fair, but it is the only life you have to live and it is your responsibility to live it to its fullest. The only person you can control is yourself.

In his book *"Breaking the Spirit of Average: 7 Keys to Turn your AVERAGE into AWESOME"*, Joseph B. Washington shares a great story that highlights the importance a coach can play or having someone in your life who provides guidance and good counsel so that you won't waste time and other precious resources.

"The young man stared at the massive stone wall before him. It stood at least twenty-five feet high and easily two feet thick. It was old and weathered, and overgrown with a thick layer of tangled vines. The young man knew he had to get to the other side of this wall, but how? It stretched as far as he could see in either direction. Though running around the sides seemed like an impossible feat, he still thought it was worth a shot. If he ran fast enough, he might be able to see the end within a few minutes.

He took off with a burst of energy; his long strides propelled him forward with ease. Yet after almost half an hour of running, he had to pause for a break. He must have gone three miles at least, and still no end in sight! After a brief rest, he felt a second wind. Should he try to run back in the other direction?

After some thought, he decided to try to scale the wall. Twenty-five feet was high, but not insurmountable. This plan did not prove any easier. With every attempt the vines broke off under his weight. The sides of the wall were rough but offered no visible footholds. Another hour of determined effort found him still sitting on the ground. Discouraged and exhausted, the young man picked up a small stone and began the arduous task of chipping away at the wall itself. Maybe some of the stones would pry loose, he thought. Even though the thoughts of burrowing through a wall that thick was depressing to say the least, it seemed to be his only hope.

After many hours of chipping away, an old man comes by. He was not particularly impressive to look at, but his face had a pleasant and peaceful look. He stood off to the side and watched the young man hard at work for a while before calling to him gently and offering a bottle of water. After graciously thanking the old man for the water, the young man took a sip and then turned back to his hopeless tunneling. The old man put his hand on the young man's shoulder and beckoned him to follow. Tired, but curious, the young man followed.

About fifty yards away, the man pointed to a spot on the wall. He began pulling the vines away, and the young man joined in helping him. A few minutes later, the small clearing revealed a weathered wooden door. The hinges were rusted over, and there was no handle. With a couple of pushes it began to give away. The young man stared thankfully at the old man who had come to his aid. Now what seemed like a major obstacle to him getting to the other side was only a shove away."

Stop making the same decisions with the belief that the outcome will somehow turnout different. It will not. We are emotional creatures and emotions are good and serve a very specific purpose; however, all too often some allow their emotions alone to dictate the decisions they make and it is never a good idea to base a decision on just pure emotions alone.

Exercise 14: In the space below, write down three goals you have been putting off for sometime.

_____

_____

_____

_____

_____

_____

_____

_____

_____

_____

_____

_____

_____

_____

Exercise 15: For the goals you listed above, write down the reasons why you have been putting them off and be specific.

_____
_____
_____
_____
_____
_____
_____
_____
_____
_____
_____
_____
_____
_____

Exercise 16: Write down reasons why these goals are important to you and be specific.

Exercise 17: If the reasons why you keep putting the goal off out weighs how important the goal is to you, come up with another goal.

If the reason why the goal is important to you outweighs the reason why you have been putting it off, get started immediately doing what it takes to accomplish that goal.

Chapter 7

Conclusion

The number 7 is symbolic with completion. Now that you have made it to the end of this journey *(this book)*, hopefully you have followed the simple instructions provided when you first began reading this book and those instructions were to make sure you completed each exercise before moving on. If you didn't, go back and complete the exercises. This is where the true growth will take place. If you did complete each exercise, excellent! You should be well on your way to implementing the necessary behavior and habit modifications in your life so that your lifestyle will be one of your choosing and not one that has been handed to you.

Make sure you continue your journey to self-mastery and modeling excellence. Never stop learning and continue exposing yourself to new learning technologies and strategies regarding behavior modification and flexibility. According to statistics, the average person reads around 9 books per year. That's less than one book per month, whereas the average millionaire reads 56 books per year; that's one book per week. You and you alone are responsible for your life and the quality of it. Although things may occur on the outside of you that you may have no control of, you always have the ability to control what occurs on the inside of you.

"Whatever you vividly imagine, ardently desire, sincerely believe, and enthusiastically act upon ... must inevitably come to pass!" Paul J. Meyer

About Our Logo

Our logo is a triangle with a quadrant located in the middle of it. The triangle represents a road to infinity. This is indicative of the infinite creativity and resourcefulness of the human spirit. The quadrant in the middle, our **"Success Flow Quadrant"**, consists of 4 letters. The letters FDFS represent Fear, Desire, Freedom and Security. Fear and Desire make up the left side of the quadrant and Freedom and Security make up the right side of the quadrant.

Most spend their entire lives on the left side of the quadrant toggling back-and-forth between Fear and Desire. Those who are willing to fight for what they truly Desire, embrace change, stay focused and not quit make the transition to the Freedom and Security side of the quadrant. When it all comes down to it, people only want 2 things in life ... the Freedom to control their lives as they see fit and make their own decisions and the Security of knowing they as well as their loved-ones are Secure in every aspect of their lives.

Due to Fear, most never accomplish what they truly want to accomplish, but if their Desire to achieve that thing becomes greater than their Fear of facing it, a major breakthrough can happen!

www.ingramcontent.com/pod-product-compliance
Lightning Source LLC
Chambersburg PA
CBHW050655160426
43194CB00010B/1948